THE Power OF THE SACRAMENTS

SR BRIEGE MᶜKENNA OSC

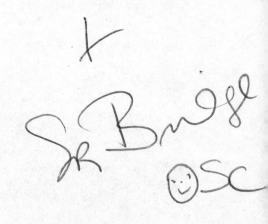

VERITAS

First published 2009 by
Veritas Publications
7/8 Lower Abbey Street
Dublin 1
Ireland
Email publications@veritas.ie
Website www.veritas.ie

ISBN 978 1 84730 170 3

10 9 8 7 6 5 4 3 2

A catalogue record for this book is available from the British
Library.

Cover design by Lir Mac Cárthaigh
Book design and typesetting by Colette Dower
Printed in the Republic of Ireland by Hudson Killeen Ltd, Dublin

Veritas books are printed on paper made from the wood pulp of
managed forests. For every tree felled, at least one tree is planted,
thereby renewing natural resources.

CONTENTS

INTRODUCTION

The sacraments are so much a part of our Catholic life that sometimes we take them for granted. If we take the time to think about them, we will better understand what a great treasure our Lord gave us in them. Then we will revitalise our faith and profit more from the sacraments. Instead of falling into routine, each sacrament we receive will become more and more of a personal meeting with Jesus.

In life we set out on two journeys. The first begins at the moment of conception, that extraordinary moment when our parents impart life to us. We plunge into a physical journey. When we gaze at an infant, we realise that only God could breathe life into it. On this physical journey God in his providence provides everything we require: eyes, hands, head, heart. God in his goodness provides what we take for granted. He enables the mother to supply those needs during the nine months she knits a child in the womb. Throughout the life of the child, and into adulthood, God continues to give us all we need.

So we continue on our physical journey and we begin our spiritual journey. God allows us to glimpse insights into nature and we discover wonders. Through research and medical science, we uncover gifts that benefit our physical bodies. This all comes from God. God has given us the gifts of science and medicine to help us on the journey of life. The book of Sirach bids us to honour physicians, and recognise that God gives them to us to help us (cf. Sirach 38:1-2). Sometimes we take them for granted. We also know that we should take care of our bodies. We agonise over the poor people when famine strikes. Their bodies shrivel and wither because they do not have enough food to eat. Some people blame this on God and wonder, 'Why would God let this happen?' But human greed causes it to happen. The earth can supply enough food to feed everybody but so often people exploit each other.

God also provides for our spiritual journey. Once, on a radio show, someone asked me a question: 'What about the pagans? Will all those people who have not been baptised be saved?' Yes, they can be saved. It is not the people who have never heard about God that I anguish over. It is the people who hear the saving word of God and reject it. It is the people like us who come from countries that once treasured the faith. Our ancestors entrusted the faith to us and we spurn it through materialism and ungodliness. God will call us to account for this.

THE SACRAMENT
OF BAPTISM

God provides for us on this spiritual journey. The first and greatest sacrament that we receive is the sacrament of Baptism. In this sacrament God adopts us and snatches us from the darkness of original sin. The sacrament of Baptism does something similar to what a family does when it adopts a little boy or girl. The family goes through a legal process to change the child's name to the name of that family. That child then has a right to everything the family has. To be adopted means to become a member of the family. In the case of children who are born into their natural families, through the beautiful gift that comes from parenthood, the mother and father know the child and it resembles them. But in the case of the youngster who was adopted, we say it is a child of the heart. I heard this beautiful definition of adoption from a priest in South America. A little boy confided to him, 'Mommy told me that she didn't get me out of her womb. I came out of her heart because I am adopted.'

At Baptism the Heavenly Father adopts all of us. That's why we say we are the family of God. The sacraments, as one of the old writers put it, are 'the veins of the Church'. Veins of the physical body pump blood to the heart and revitalise it. Veins run through the Church that Christ instituted when he said, 'You are Peter and on this rock I will build my Church.' The sacraments are veins that flow with life. At every stage of our spiritual journey they bring us life. What kind of life? Supernatural life, the life of grace which makes us holy. Baptism brings us into that place where we receive this life.

How can we effectively live out our Baptism? We can renew it. We were carried to the baptismal font. Perhaps we don't remember that commitment, but now each one of us can rekindle it as we get older.

I recall a beautiful testimony of a mother in Florida whose son had renounced the Church. He had turned away and for years she never heard from him. One day a priest asked this mother, 'Is your son baptised?' She said, 'Yes, certainly he's baptised.' 'So do you know what I want you to do?' He told her, 'Get the formula of Baptism, the whole baptismal ceremony. Go through it and renew the baptismal promises in your son's name. Renew the promises to renounce Satan and all his evil works. Do that for your son every time you pray for him. Claim the power of the sacrament of his Baptism. Ask Christ, who sees your son wherever he is in the world, to stir up within him the grace of his Baptism.'

Three weeks later, in the middle of the night, this boy phoned his mother. He sobbed, 'Mum, I don't know how to describe what has happened to me.' Then he related that he had met someone in a store who had invited him to a prayer meeting. In that atmosphere he had rediscovered his faith. She realised that this had happened at the time that she claimed him into the family of God again.

Today the Church warns people that if they desire Baptism for their child, then they have the great obligation to raise that child in the faith. They must give the child the opportunity to know and to experience God's life. The tragedy is that many are baptised but their ongoing religious formation is neglected.

Baptism is the most precious gift we can receive. If we pray, God will fan into flame the graces we received with this sacrament.

THE SACRAMENT
OF RECONCILIATION

As we continue our journey, sooner or later we may encounter illness. Many kinds of sickness afflict us. When travelling, we may find ourselves in a place where effective treatment is not available. So we take medications with us when we travel; when we do get ill, we go to a doctor, which is a great gift.

We can also get spiritually sick. All the sacraments have their sources in Scripture. What was the very first gift that Jesus bestowed on the disciples after the resurrection? Jesus breathed on the disciples and gave them the power to forgive sins (John 20:19-23). It is this power that the Church makes available in the Sacrament of Reconciliation or Confession. In this sacrament our sins are forgiven, our sicknesses are healed. In this sacrament we experience healing and wholeness and the tenderness of God's divine mercy.

The secular pyschologised world we live in tries to deceive us into thinking that there really is no such thing as sin. Society insinuates this in a variety of ways: 'Well, it's no harm'; 'It is really not a sin.' But we have to ask, 'Why then did Jesus suffer and die on the cross?' St John affirmed that if we say we don't sin, we are liars and we make God a liar (1 John 1:10).

God sent his Son into the world to save us and to redeem us from sin. Knowing that we would sin, he gave us a sacrament to forgive sin. We are baptised once. We don't need to be adopted ten times, we just need to be adopted once. However, we frequently fall into sin. Jesus gave us the Sacrament of Reconciliation to cure that sickness. We come to the priest, but it is not the priest who grants us forgiveness, but Christ acting through him. By sin, we can't hurt God. Christ is risen now and he can't suffer anymore. By sin we hurt each other. Look at the pain that sin causes in the world. Our sins affect other people. We live together and we affect each other for good and for bad. In our society sin blights entire communities. When people rob, murder and rape, that sin, that evil, devastates us. God in his great wisdom has given us this sacrament through the Church. He asks us to humble ourselves. He declared to the first ordained priests, 'I will empower you. When people confess their sins, I will forgive them through you' (Cf. John 20:19).

Today people *are* going to confession – but in pubs, to the bartender; in beauty salons, to the hairdresser. On planes, I hear confessions from people all the time. But the bartender can't absolve them, the hairdresser can't give absolution and I can't give it, although I can certainly pray. The Sacrament of Reconciliation liberates us from sin and guilt. People pay to see psychiatrists, and psychiatrists are good, but they cannot give us what Jesus gives. A sacrament imparts divine grace. It is an outward sign of an inward grace. When we confess our sins, we need to have real sorrow and resolve with God's help not to sin again.

What does the sacrament do? It fortifies us against sin and it opens our eyes that were blind. It also heals people who are spiritually sick. We're all going to die. Our bodies are going to die, but our souls will never die. We'll get new bodies. What happens to our bodies here doesn't matter. The Lord told us that we will get new bodies, but we won't get new souls. The soul is immortal. We're only on a pilgrimage here. This helps us realise why the Lord in his mercy and great love gave us sacraments that are guaranteed. He promises, 'I will be there to help you'. That's what a sacrament is. In the sacraments Christ guarantees his presence. This doesn't depend on feelings; it depends on faith. On each step of our journey he meets us with the needs we have.

My co-worker, Father Kevin Scallon CM, and I tell many extraordinary stories of what happened to people who went to confession. Once when we were giving a retreat in the United States, we were asked to speak to a parish community during a mission. On the first night of the mission we explained to the people that we were not going to be talking only about physical healing. What good is it to have a healthy body when your soul is shrouded in darkness, sin and despair? The first night the theme was repentance. About seventeen priests gathered that night. We spoke about penance, confession, sin and the commandments. Sin is still sin. The Vatican Council did not abolish sin. It did not change the Gospel or the commandments, or the Beatitudes or the teachings in Matthew, chapter 5.

When we had confession that night, I'm sure that many people came there to be physically healed. They knew that Sister Briege was going to be there and they wanted me to pray over them. Two days later, a woman called up excitedly and asked to talk to Father Kevin. She told him, 'Father, my husband and I brought our little girl to the prayer service because she has dyslexia. We hoped Sister Briege would pray with us for healing.' But that night we didn't have a prayer service for physical healing. Instead, we had this beautiful sacrament. The woman went on to say:

> That night I was sitting in the sanctuary directing all these people to the real healing power in the sacrament. I was telling them which priests were available. My husband and I went to confession too. My husband is a polio victim, but that has never hindered him from living a normal life. He has a good job as president of a bank. We didn't intend

to ask for healing for him. But what happened astounded us. Yesterday when he was on his way to lunch from the office, his leg began to tingle. Then last night when he undressed to go to bed, he saw that muscle had grown in his leg. By the end of the week he had two perfect legs. His polio-withered leg was completely restored.

I never saw that man. Father Kevin saw him only in the Sacrament of Reconciliation. But just as that whole parish did, the woman and her husband realised that every sacrament is a meeting with the Risen Jesus. The Risen Jesus healed that man for reasons we will never know. He not only said, 'Yes, I forgive your sins,' but he said, 'Get up and walk'. Many people forget that meeting with Jesus to ask for healing of sickness of soul will also bring great healing to the body and the mind. Jesus knew that, and that's why he gave us the sacrament: to heal us on our journey.

During the first night of every parish mission that Father Kevin and I give there is a call to repentance with the Sacrament of Reconciliation. Usually there are many priests available to hear confessions. On one occasion at a parish mission, a gentleman who had gone to confession phoned Father Kevin the next day to tell him that he had returned to his doctor, who only a few weeks prior had diagnosed him with lung cancer, to find out that he was cancer-free. He was so excited because he had realised that it was during the Sacrament of Reconciliation that something wonderful had happened in both his soul and his body. It reminds us of the man's encounter with Jesus who was lowered through the roof. Jesus looked at his soul, forgave his sins and then told him to get up and walk (Mark 2:1-12).

The great thing about the Catholic Church is that it is a Church of sinners. We can say that about every one of us who belongs to it. A man once confronted one of the bishops of Northern Ireland with the fact that the Catholic Church buries people who are involved in violent political activity. He blamed the Church for offering Mass for people who belong to paramilitary groups. I thought the bishop's answer bespoke the wisdom of God. The bishop replied that the Catholic Church is full of sinners. The Mass implores the mercy of God and the redeeming blood of Christ. Jesus told us not to judge one another.

Who can refuse the mercy of God? Jesus doesn't. But sometimes this is hard for us to grasp in our human way of thinking. We fail to understand that if the worst murderer or the worst rapist kneels before the Lord and confesses, God forgives him. Look at St Paul: he persecuted Christians, yet in one instant God transformed him.

Peter denied Jesus. He insisted, 'I don't know Jesus Christ! I don't know him!' Yet God forgave him. Others like St Ignatius and St Augustine wallowed in sin before they came to the Lord. The tremendous truth about our God is that when he forgives, he forgets. It is hard for us to understand such great mercy.

We have to confront sin and darkness. We cannot stand and judge others as if we are not sinners. None of us can throw the first stone. I have to go to confession. I confess every week, not just as a devotion, but because I need it. The world we live in tempts us to sin. Apostasy is rampant and people try to undermine our faith in Jesus Christ. Our society condones much that is evil. 'It's all right,' it whispers, 'after all, you're only human.' But through Baptism we become the children of God. So we strive to be perfect human beings.

THE SACRAMENT OF EUCHARIST

Chapter 6 of St John's Gospel tells about Jesus' teaching on the bread of life. But many of the people listening could not accept what he was saying. Some of the saddest lines in the whole Gospel come at the end of this passage. Jesus turned to the disciples, the men whom he had chosen, and he posed the question, 'Do you want to leave me?' It was easy for them to follow Jesus when they saw signs and wonders. But he was inviting them to believe not with bodily eyes but with inner eyes. He was calling them to believe with their hearts. But many failed because they couldn't accept the word of God and they went away.

In today's world and even within the Church, many people compromise the Gospel. They rationalise the teachings of Christ and the teachings of the Church. Even some of those who are called to preach the word of God are afraid to speak out. They are terrified to lose people and they protest, 'We can't preach that because people won't come to church'. Or they argue, 'If we proclaim the Catholic Church's teachings on birth control, we might lose them'.

Yet this passage of the St John's Gospel is very consoling. The teaching on the bread of life was so difficult for them to accept because Jesus was standing there in his physical body. He was a man with flesh and blood. He gave them this profound teaching that he intended to give himself to them to eat. They couldn't grasp it because they took it literally, in the sense of his physical body that they could see. He declared, 'I'm going to give you my flesh to eat and my blood to drink'. It's as if someone were to stand up in front of a group of people and say, 'Because I love all of you people so much I'm going to give myself to you to eat'. People would think, 'That person is crazy'. But when people flocked to Jesus, this is what he told them. He didn't retract it because he meant it.

The marvel is that the Lord did intend to give himself. In his risen presence he would lavish himself in a way that can be accepted only through faith. As the *Catechism of the Catholic Church* tells us:

> It is by the conversion of the bread and wine into Christ's body and blood that Christ becomes present in this sacrament ... Thus St John Chrysostom declares: 'It is not man that causes the things offered to become the Body and Blood of Christ, but he who was crucified for us, Christ himself. The priest, in the role of Christ, pronounces these words, but their power and grace are God's. This is my body, he says. This word transforms the things offered.' (202)

Some people doubt this, and will not be convinced no matter how much we try. To profess faith in the real presence of Christ and to recognise the value of this sacrament is a gift of God. To recognise the value of the sacraments is a gift of God. As he watched them go, Jesus didn't shout, 'Come back, I didn't mean what I said'. Instead, he let them go. Then he challenged the twelve, those men whom he was going to empower, and he gave them a choice. Jesus said to the twelve, 'Will you also go away?" (John 6:67).

It is good to recall that although Jesus was kind and compassionate, he did make demands. He demanded that if the apostles love him, they must believe him. We must believe in Jesus too. Peter answered for us when he said to Jesus, 'Lord, to whom shall we go? You have the words of eternal life and we have believed, and have come to know, that you are the holy one of God' (John 6:68-70).

We need food on our journey. Jesus knew that we would need spiritual food too. So what did he do? He instituted the Blessed Eucharist. Think about that first Holy Thursday night. Jesus knew that he had to fulfil his mission that week. He knew that he would suffer horribly, yet the world's salvation depended on it. He would face his greatest agony and he would show his love by giving everything. Yet his humanity cried out, 'O God if it's possible take it away from me' (Mark

14:35-37). Knowing that he was going to his death, he thought of how we would respond to his love.

God cares about us. He sent his Son to teach us how to live and to show us how to interact in society. Jesus showed us how to act towards our enemies and those who oppose us. Jesus gave us a road map and told us, 'If you follow my way, you'll have freedom. If the Son sets you free, you will truly be free'. He also promised, 'I will give you myself to eat. I will be your food on this journey'. How? We could not eat his physical body. Only God could have thought of this wondrous mystery. He took something very humble, bread and wine. It is important for us to go back to the Gospel and ponder what Jesus said. Jesus knew from the start those who would refuse to believe. But he taught about this great mystery, 'I am the bread of life. I will give myself to you. Those who eat my flesh and drink my blood will have life' (Cf. John 6). He was not just talking about physical life, because many people are physically alive but spiritually dead. Many people live only on a human level. They have never experienced what it means to be alive. This is why the Church as a Mother obliges us to go to church on Sunday. The Church urges us to go to Mass to hear the Word of God and receive the Bread of Life. A mother wants her child to have food even if the child doesn't want to eat it. The mother knows the child needs it. The Church is a mother. So the Church puts an obligation on us, not because Christ needs us but because we need him.

The Church calls us to live according to the teachings of Christ. Scripture says that we cannot eat the body and blood of Christ and at the same time refuse to believe and to follow his teachings. It is a contradiction. So we pray and tell Jesus that we desire his life which comes to us through the Church and the Sacraments. The Church guides us on our spiritual journey. But the devil doesn't want us to listen to the Church. Today people seek a religion of their own making – a 'smorgasbord religion', 'they pick and choose what they want'! That is why sin has seeped in everywhere. We don't have the strength to resist sin if we deprive ourselves of this bread of life, the food for our journey.

As Catholics, what do we believe about the Eucharist? We Catholics shouldn't be afraid that we might offend others if we proclaim what we believe. We believe that the Eucharist, the Paschal Mystery, is the making present of the passion, death and resurrection of Christ. At every Eucharist in every Catholic Church anywhere in the world, we believe that we find the two tables: the table of the living Word of God and the table of the Eucharist.

The Catholic Church has always proclaimed the Word of God to its people all over the world. That is the table of the Word. When a bishop is ordained, the Book of the Gospels is placed upon his head. The Church commissions him, and through him and his priests, to proclaim the Word of God.

We also partake of the table of the Eucharist. Through the ministry of the priest, the Church renews Christ's sacrifice of Calvary in an un-bloody way. We *re*-present Christ's passion, death and resurrection to the Father. On Holy Thursday night, Jesus with his disciples celebrated the Pascal Mystery, the First Eucharist. He took the bread and wine, said the prayer of blessing, gave it to his disciples saying, 'This is my body ... this is my blood,' the sacrifice of the new and eternal covenant.

The Apostles ate and drank Christ's body and blood. Jesus imparted to them the grace of his own priesthood and commanded them, 'Do this in memory of me'. From that night, to this very day, the line of the priesthood in the Church has never been broken. Even in times of tremendous darkness, even when persecution broke out, God always protected his Church. A remnant always remained steadfast. In her history, the Church has experienced both Christ's passion and his resurrection.

The National Day of Prayer for Priests at Knock Shrine was founded by Father Kevin

Scallon. One year, among the thousands of people in attendance, was a young Protestant mother whose child was dying. She had been encouraged by a Catholic friend to visit Knock on that day and ask me to pray with her for her child. She had never visited the Republic of Ireland before and certainly had never been to anything Catholic, but she was desperate for her child, who was so critically ill and dying in a Belfast hospital, that she informed her husband that she was going to meet me. After arriving at Knock and seeing the crowds of people, she knew there was no possibility of personally praying with me. During the Eucharistic Service, she heard me speaking about the real presence of Jesus in the Eucharist; that 'this is Jesus in the host' and that 'it is Jesus who heals'. And while she didn't fully understand what it meant, she did have a great faith in Jesus; and as she saw others doing, she stretched out her arms towards the host and said, 'If this is you Jesus, please heal my little daughter'. To her great surprise, when she returned home, her husband greeted her with excitement, telling her that their daughter had taken an unexpected turn for the better and that the doctors were going to release her from the hospital for her to return home. This reminds us that it is the same Jesus present in the Eucharist who told the Centurion to go home and his servant would be healed (Matthew 8:5-13).

All spiritual growth takes place because of the Eucharist. As Vatican II stated, 'The liturgy is the summit toward which the activity of the Church is directed; at the same time it is the font from which all her power flows' (*Constitution on the Sacred Liturgy*, no. 10).

We should ponder the reality of this great sacrament. What is it? We believe that when we receive Communion we receive the living bread of life, the body and blood of Christ. Please ask yourself as a Catholic, 'Do I really believe?' People will say that such a thing is impossible. But in this sacrament, in the Mass, we meet the Risen Christ who is really and truly present in that Sacred Host. When we take the Host, we receive the risen Christ. If we believe that, why don't we crowd into our churches? Why are so many people depressed? Why are they mentally, spiritually and physically ill? Could it be that we don't really believe? Could it be that we have only come to fulfil our obligations but we haven't realised we can find healing? Christ heals us and gives us the strength we need to go out and fight sin in the world. The Eucharist gives us this strength.

THE SACRAMENT
OF CONFIRMATION

When we go from church to the supermarket or the office, we may meet people who totally oppose Christ's way. Every day, every week, we need the strength of Christ to keep us on the right path. We cannot deceive ourselves into thinking that the corruption of sin will not contaminate us. It would be like going into a plague-infested area and saying, 'I won't catch the disease'. It would be naïve. Look at what television brings into our homes. What we accept today would have shocked our grandparents. The media glamorises immorality such as young people living together, having pre-marital sex. It glorifies adultery – people who become intimate with someone else's husband or wife. We think nothing of marrying two, three or four times. We tolerate corruption in business and government. Parents are sometimes afraid to speak out and condemn such a lifestyle as contrary to the teachings of Christ. We may start to think that it must be all right since 'everybody's doing it'. That's why only those families that have a strong Catholic Christian life will escape unharmed. We need each other's support. That's why we talk about the body of Christ. That's why we need to recognise that we must support each other in a world that opposes the Gospel.

So that we can meet these challenges, we have another sacrament – Confirmation. What does it do for us on our journey? At a certain age in a young person's life, he or she will have to face a world that is hostile to Christ. The apostles faced this challenge. For them it was easy when they were with Jesus. But Jesus knew that they would tremble when opposition arose. So what did he do? He instructed them, 'Wait here, and I will bestow on you the power of the Spirit'. So the Holy Spirit came upon them and they became completely convinced of what they said. That is why Peter could gaze on the beggar at the temple gate, who hoped to get gold, and declare, 'I don't have silver and gold, but I have Jesus Christ' (Cf. Acts 3). The Holy Spirit empowered them to go out and preach. When the authorities flogged and imprisoned the apostles, they retorted, 'We will not obey you. We cannot obey, for we have to speak of what we know and what we have seen'. They proclaimed Christ through the power of the Holy Spirit. Confirmation is a sacrament that strengthens and energises Christians to be heralds of Jesus Christ.

That sounds wonderful, but how many of us call upon the power of this sacrament into our lives? How many of us recognise that this sacrament is like a new Pentecost? It is the Pentecost of our lives when the bishop, with the outward sign, confirms us in our faith. Then all the winds of false doctrines will not shake our faith.

I met Father Phil Crosby in Korea. He wrote a book called *Three Winters' Cold*. It's about his march through North Korea when the communists took over. He impressed me very much. He was a priest deeply committed to the teachings of Christ and the Church. Every morning Father Kevin and I went into chapel at five o'clock in the morning to spend some hours before the Blessed Sacrament. This wonderful Columban missionary priest was always there with his eyes riveted on the tabernacle. He stayed for our retreat and I talked with him afterward. What struck me about him and his book was the strength God gave him to cling to his priesthood. In the winters they marched through the snow and ice as their captors beat them. He recalled the young American GIs, who looked like skeletons as they trudged by. They pleaded with the bishop and the priests who were marching there, 'Please, give us absolution'. They confessed their sins because they recognised their need for forgiveness. Father Crosby said that what mattered for him as a priest was to have the strength to endure and not to abandon the struggle.

Once we gave a retreat to a group of Chinese priests. One of them had spent twenty-six years in chains. He had to eat off the floor like a dog. He was persecuted because he would not compromise his Catholic priesthood. This beautiful old Chinese priest told me, 'Sister Briege, it is only when you experience persecution that you can understand how much God strengthens you. Today, I thank God that I had the privilege to spend twenty-six years in chains, not for some trivial cause, but for the Gospel of Jesus Christ.' We don't have to face what he faced. Perhaps the greatest grace would be to suffer persecution for the faith.

What then is the grace of Confirmation? This sacrament strengthens us to stand up for Christ. How easy it is to stand up and deny Christ. We deny Christ when we say that it's all right to have sex outside of marriage. We deny Christ when we say that it's all right to take drugs. We deny Christ when we say that it's all right to have an abortion. To deny Christ is to choose the ways of the world and taunt Christ, 'You and your teachings are not important'. Jesus gave us the Sacrament of Confirmation to fortify us with the power of His Holy Spirit.

When the charismatic renewal began, it focused on the Holy Spirit. The Spirit has always been in the Church. But Pope John XXIII begged God to shower us with a new outpouring of the Spirit. The Pope urged the universal Church to pray for a new Pentecost. We got the new Pentecost and many of us were afraid of it! We didn't know what to make of it. We shied away from it. But the Holy Spirit started to stir the hearts of simple believers, like those people I meet in Latin America. They may not read or write, but they can get up and evangelise because the Spirit of God inspires them. Christ bestowed on us the gift of the Holy Spirit to accompany us on our journey. When you hear some people tear down and criticise the Church, ask yourself, 'What kind of a Catholic am I? Do I defend and proclaim Christ or am I ashamed or embarrassed to do so?' The Sacrament of Confirmation will fortify us in all the challenges of life.

THE SACRAMENT OF MARRIAGE

Christ also gave us the Sacrament of Matrimony. This sacrament seals the love of two people. This sacrament enables a couple, through their union as husband and wife, to cement their love in Christ. The priest witnesses the sacrament of a couple, but he doesn't marry them. The man and woman marry each other.

Marriage is like a river that flows with graces from the moment a couple approach the altar and kneel together before it. They say, 'Christ, we want to invite you into our lives. We want you to be with us'. The spouses are not alone in their marriage; Christ is with them. From the first day of the sacrament, a river of graces flows out from Christ – through sufferings, through good times and bad, through sickness and death. There is no limit to these graces. It's like drinking from a fountain. The couple can always turn to Christ to renew the sacramental grace of marriage.

In today's Church we need to recognise the sacredness of marriage. Christ knew how difficult marriage would be. It involves two people who come from different backgrounds and grow into a close union. This growth happens in many ways. Christ is always there when married people need him.

I once had a beautiful experience that showed me the power of this sacrament. Some years ago, someone approached me and said, 'Briege, there's a man here who wants to talk to you. He's not physically sick, but says he's desperate'. I said that I would meet with him. So this very striking man, about thirty-five, came to see me. (I'll call him Jim.) He was the president and owner of a big company, so he was financially very well off. He was a good man, a daily communicant, who had been brought up in a staunch Catholic family. I showed him into the chapel. As he came in, Jim broke down and cried, 'I'm desperate'. Then he related his story to me. He said, 'Sister, I've been married for fifteen years. I have a beautiful wife and three beautiful children. But something terrible just happened. About a week ago I decided to come home early from the office. When I walked in, the phone rang so I picked it up. But my wife was already on the line and I heard her speaking. She was making a date with another man. I thought; *it can't be*. I couldn't believe this was happening to us because we had a good marriage. We've had a good sexual relationship and I thought everything was fine.'

Then he told me that he approached his wife about it when she hung up but she refused to discuss it. To think that his wife was seeing someone else devastated him. For the next few weeks she still refused to talk about it. Jim knew that she was seeing the other man once a week, and all she would say about it was, 'I'm just trying to help him'. Jim sought advice from a marriage counsellor who told him, 'Give her an ultimatum and then leave her if she doesn't change'.

I will never forget how he looked when he came to me. He knelt before the Blessed Sacrament and sobbed, 'Sister Briege, I love my wife. I know my marriage is sacred before God. Isn't there anything I can do to save it? I believe in the sacrament and I don't want to leave her. I love her.'

I looked at this good man and didn't know what to say. So I prayed, 'Jesus, please tell me what to say to him'. A voice from the tabernacle said to me, 'Tell him it may get worse, but it will get better. Tell him that I'm with him and will sustain him with the grace of the sacrament. Tell him not to give up.' When I related this to Jim, he just stared at me, as if he could not cope with it.

Every week for the next ten months, he travelled a long way to see me. The only thing he ever did was sit in the chapel. I would pray, and he would just sit there and talk. He would talk out everything on his mind and then he would ask me to pray with him. I would pray with him and encourage him not to give up.

It turned out that his wife's lover had a spiritist working on the marriage to destroy it. We see a tremendous rise today in witchcraft, spiritism and all kinds of forces of evil. The spiritist wrote to Jim and told him, 'I met your wife in another realm of life. She's really not yours so you'll have to let her go. This marriage has to break up.' Jim showed me these letters, which also referred to séance groups. Every time I heard about this, I kept getting the message inside me, 'Greater is he that is within you than he that is in the world'. So I encouraged him, 'Don't give in; you have Jesus with you. You are married and have the graces of the sacrament. You go to Mass every day. You will win the battle.'

All this time his wife would still not talk to him about it, which caused him great distress. But he still went to Mass and he never condemned her. There are many hidden saints in the Church. Jim knew that when he was out working, his wife went every week to see the other man. Jim would beg God to give her the grace to turn away from the temptation to betray her marriage commitment.

He phoned me one night when I was in Europe. He confided, 'Briege, the affair, it's all over. I just want to thank you for the way you've supported me through this.' So I thought that God had used me to help him get through this difficult phase of his life, but not that it was over.

About three months later I was getting ready to go on a trip and I was doing something very simple – brushing my teeth. As I looked up it was as if God showed me a picture of Jim in the mirror and said, 'Phone him today'. So I called him. He explained, 'Sister, I was just about to phone you.

Can I come and talk to you?' So that day he came to see me. As he came into the chapel, he sank into a pew and put his head down. He begged, 'Please pray with me. I can't tell you anything. But if God wants you to know, he'll reveal it to you, because you've helped me so much.' I heard the Lord say, 'His wife is pregnant and it's not his child'. So I looked at him and said, 'Jim, your wife is going to have a child'. He looked at me and nodded yes.

I asked, 'When did you find out? How do you feel?' He replied, 'Sister, my wife told me a short time after she broke off with the other man'. I questioned him again, 'How do you feel?' He took my hands in his and began to weep. 'Sister Briege,' he said, 'if Jesus can forgive me every time I sin, how can I not forgive my wife? When she told me this, I assured her that I would accept the child as my own and that I forgave her.' I asked, 'How did she respond?' He replied, 'She looked at me. Her mouth dropped open and she exclaimed: "If you, a human being that I have hurt so deeply, can do this, what must God be like?"'

Then Jim said, 'I now realise that if it weren't for the grace of this sacrament, and if it weren't for your encouragement, I would be divorced.' He added with a smile, 'Just pray that the little child will look like me.'

A beautiful thing happened. The child was born. I didn't see Jim until seven years later, at a football game. I was with some of our students who were playing. Jim's son was in the game and I saw Jim walking with a little girl. He turned around, smiled at me and pointed to the girl, who was gorgeous. I felt the Lord saying to me, 'Satan tried to break that marriage'. But God in his goodness protected and saved it, even though it's a mystery to us. Jim wrote me a letter in which he said, 'I just want to tell you that I took my marriage for granted. I thought my wife knew I loved her. I also want to thank you because I now realise that God is faithful when he said, "I will be with you."'

THE SACRAMENT
OF THE ANOINTING
OF THE SICK

Christ instituted the Sacrament of the Sick because he knew that our physical bodies would get sick. Before the Second Vatican Council, this sacrament was called Extreme Unction, and was only administered to people during their final illness. It is now called the Sacrament of the Anointing of the Sick. So what is the Sacrament of the Sick? It is not just a sacrament for the dying. The Sacrament of the Sick is a sacrament of healing. It is the healing touch of Christ that the priest brings when we are sick. It's not for minor illness, but serious sickness like cancer or arthritis, things that afflict us and bind us, and prevent us from having a full life. The priest lays his hands on the sick person and anoints him/her with holy oil. I pray a lot for healing, but I cannot celebrate this sacrament of healing. There's no comparison between my prayer and a sacrament of the Church. I can only bow in the presence of the healing, consoling Christ. Every sacrament makes Christ present. When the priest anoints us, Christ assures us, 'I am healing you'.

Many healings have taken place through this holy anointing. People with cancer and leukaemia have been healed through the Sacrament of the Sick. It is becoming more alive in the Church again. On the physical level we're learning about all the ways that the body can be healed. On the spiritual level the Church is rediscovering many of her own treasures. The seven sacraments have always been there. The Church guided by the Holy Spirit is bringing new life to God's people through them. The Sacrament of the Sick is not just for people who are dying. It's for people who are alive. It heals us on many levels. As with every encounter with Christ, we need to have a living, expectant faith in the power of Jesus to heal us.

I once met a priest who had surgery and was very distressed because he had a terrible wound that wouldn't heal. A nurse would come every second day to dress the wound. During a priest retreat given by Father Kevin and myself, the priest came forward for the Sacrament of the Anointing of the Sick. He wasn't aware of anything physically happening at the time, but to his great surprise when the dressing was removed that same evening, the wound was healed and only a scar remained.

On another occasion, a priest had returned to Ireland from the missions because he was suffering from malaria. The doctor told him he was never going to be able to return to the missions. He came to the 'Intercession for Priests', received the Sacrament of the Anointing of the Sick, and, at that moment, felt the power of Jesus heal him. He was able to return to the missions for many more years of priestly ministry.

When I attended a Divine Mercy evening in a parish church some years ago, a six-year-old boy approached me and informed me that his grandmother had sent him to ask me to ask Jesus to heal him. I spoke with the child and told him that the priest would be carrying Jesus around the church in the monstrance, explaining that it is Jesus who heals. At the end of Mass, the priest told me of a very interesting encounter with the little boy. He explained that this child stepped into the aisle, put his hand up motioning him to stop, and then began speaking to Jesus, telling Him his story and asking Jesus to heal him. Two weeks later, the little boy's grandmother wrote to me saying that when this child was two years of age he had had a kidney removed due to cancer, and now at age six was to have the other kidney removed for the same reason. His prognosis was very bleak. But praise God, when he returned to the doctor two days after the Mass, it was discovered that his kidney was healed as good as new. A few years later I met the same little boy. Now radiant, his words to me were, 'Jesus is brilliant. I am all better'. He had made his First Holy Communion and he was completely healed: a wonderful example of the power of Jesus in the Blessed Sacrament to heal and of the faith of the child to believe.

THE SACRAMENT
OF HOLY ORDERS

The Sacrament of Holy Orders makes it possible for us to receive all the other sacraments. If we compare the sacraments to veins that run through the Church, this is the main artery. If we did not have this sacrament, we would not have bishops and priests, and we would not have the other sacraments.

The devil is the father of lies. He knows that if he can attack the priesthood it affects the whole Church. A priest is a human being, a man with sins, who is just as human as the rest of us. Satan wants to demoralise us. Catholics are foolish when they tear down the priesthood, because it affects all of us. The Sacrament of Holy Orders is the sacrament that is given to men so that they in turn will bring the divine life to the faithful.

The priesthood is not a job. It is not a profession. It's a gift. It has nothing to do with equality. It doesn't make priests better than the rest of us. They are still men, still 'vessels of clay' (2 Cor 4:7). But we have to reverence the sacredness of their calling. They serve at the table of the Lord, proclaiming the Word of God. They minister to us in a wonderful way. The devil hates them because they are more powerful than he. Jesus didn't say to the angels nor to anyone else what he said to the apostles. Jesus did not confer on anyone else His own power and authority. Even if the priest is sinful and weak, even if he may not be living a life worthy of his calling, when he ministers the sacraments they are still valid. We can get confused about this. We forget it and we judge the Church. Remember that the priest is only an instrument. Sometimes you hear people say, 'I don't like the priest, so I do not go to Mass'. That's like saying, 'I don't like the plate the food is on, so I will not eat'.

We need the priest as the channel that God has given us. God gives the priest power, but not to dominate others. Bishops and priests have the right to speak with authority. When I give them retreats, I tell them that they don't have to apologise for the teachings of Christ. Today the Church needs priests and bishops who proclaim the truth boldly. We need to pray for this; pray that bishops and priests will not be afraid to challenge those who teach what's contrary to Christ.

During his papacy, Pope John Paul II continually encouraged the faithful to pray for vocations to the priesthood. We see this new springtime of which he spoke happening in the lives of many who are devoted to the Eucharist and who answer the call to follow Christ.

Father Kevin and myself, when visiting seminaries, are amazed at how many men, lots of them professionals, tell us that during Eucharistic adoration they have heard the call to priesthood, to leave everything and to follow the Lord.

Pope Benedict has continuously encouraged Eucharistic adoration and intercession for priestly vocations. And thank God, many dioceses throughout the world are bearing great fruit. I have witnessed that where there is Eucharistic adoration and intercession for vocations to priesthood and religious life, it is happening, and I am continuously encouraging the laity to intercede for vocations to priesthood and religious life.

Pope Benedict has been calling men to listen and respond to the vocation of priesthood. So many hesitate because of fears, and in today's society there are many distractions and discouragements that often men fail to respond to the Lord's invitation.

I had an interesting encounter with a young man named John who was concerned for a priest friend of his. He asked to bring this priest to meet with me. I prayed with him and afterwards offered to pray with John himself. I was so surprised when I received a prophetic word for John that Jesus was calling John to priesthood and that he must not be afraid. Nothing could prevent the Lord's perfect plan except John's unwillingness to respond. John was amazed, as was I. He went on to tell me that some years past he was in a very bad marriage, was divorced and had his marriage annulled, as he should never have been married. He told me that he had heard the Lord many times and had a real desire in his heart to be a priest, but felt unworthy.

Even though his marriage was annulled, he felt he could not say yes. After receiving this word, he spoke to his spiritual director and very soon after entered the seminary. Thank God, today he is a happy priest, grateful for having responded to the Lord's call.

The powers of darkness never cease their attacks on the priesthood. We need to intercede for the Church and stand up for the teachings of the Holy Father. When Jesus said, 'You are Peter and upon this rock I will build my Church', he put Peter in authority. Pray for the Church, especially for those who have been ordained to the priesthood. Pray for these men, both bishops and priests. We live in a family, the family of God, which is the Church. It has given us everything that we need for our inner journey. Let us ask the Lord to heal us if there is something that prevents us from being happy people of God. Let us ask the Lord especially through the Eucharist to give us a new faith in his risen presence.

Let us pray:

> Loving Father, we thank you, we praise you, and we adore you for your love shown to us in Jesus our Saviour. We thank you for the many beautiful ways you call us to come to you, the source of life. We are a people who walk with Jesus on our pilgrim way. We

know our earthly journey is short. 'Seventy the sum of our years, or eighty for those who are strong' (Psalm 90:10). Father, send us your Holy Spirit to give us eyes of faith to see Jesus in the sacraments. Amen.

Mary, Mother of the Church, pray for us that the power of the risen Christ may be seen in our daily lives.